HIT SONGS FOR TWO

D0503906

Arrangements by Peter Deneff

ISBN 978-1-5400-1281-4

HAL•LEONARD®

7777 W. BLUEMOUND RD. P.O. BOX 13819 MILWAUKEE, WI 53213

For all works contained herein:
Unauthorized copying, arranging, adapting, recording, Internet posting, public performance,
or other distribution of the printed music in this publication is an infringement of copyright.
Infringers are liable under the law.

Visit Hal Leonard Online at
www.halleonard.com

CONTENTS

ALL ABOUT THAT BASS

VIOLINS

Words and Music by KEVIN KADISH
and MEGHAN TRAINOR

Copyright © 2014 Sony/ATV Music Publishing LLC, Over-Thought Under-Appreciated Songs, Year Of The Dog Music and MTrain Music
This arrangement Copyright © 2017 Sony/ATV Music Publishing LLC, Over-Thought Under-Appreciated Songs, Year Of The Dog Music and MTrain Music
All Rights on behalf of Sony/ATV Music Publishing LLC and Over-Thought Under-Appreciated Songs Administered by
Sony/ATV Music Publishing LLC, 424 Church Street, Suite 1200, Nashville, TN 37219
All Rights on behalf of Year Of The Dog Music and MTrain Music Administered by Downtown Music Publishing LLC
International Copyright Secured   All Rights Reserved

ALL OF ME

VIOLINS

Words and Music by JOHN STEPHENS
and TOBY GAD

Copyright © 2013 John Legend Publishing, EMI April Music Inc. and Gad Songs, LLC
This arrangement Copyright © 2017 John Legend Publishing, EMI April Music Inc. and Gad Songs, LLC
All Rights for John Legend Publishing Administered by BMG Rights Management (US) LLC
All Rights for EMI April Music Inc. and Gad Songs, LLC Administered by Sony/ATV Music Publishing LLC, 424 Church Street, Suite 1200, Nashville, TN 37219
All Rights Reserved   Used by Permission

BRAVE

VIOLINS

Words and Music by SARA BAREILLES
and JACK ANTONOFF

Copyright © 2013 Sony/ATV Music Publishing LLC, Tiny Bear Music and Ducky Donath Music
This arrangement Copyright © 2017 Sony/ATV Music Publishing LLC, Tiny Bear Music and Ducky Donath Music
All Rights Administered by Sony/ATV Music Publishing LLC, 424 Church Street, Suite 1200, Nashville, TN 37219
International Copyright Secured   All Rights Reserved

BUDAPEST

VIOLINS

Words and Music by GEORGE BARNETT
and JOEL POTT

Copyright © 2014 BMG Rights Management (UK) Ltd. and Chrysalis Music Ltd.
This arrangement Copyright © 2017 BMG Rights Management (UK) Ltd. and Chrysalis Music Ltd.
All Rights Administered by BMG Rights Management (US) LLC
All Rights Reserved   Used by Permission

CAN'T STOP THE FEELING

from TROLLS

VIOLINS

Words and Music by JUSTIN TIMBERLAKE,
MAX MARTIN and SHELLBACK

Copyright © 2016 by Universal Music - Z Tunes LLC, Tennman Tunes, DWA Songs and MXM
This arrangement Copyright © 2017 by Universal Music - Z Tunes LLC, Tennman Tunes, DWA Songs and MXM
All Rights for Tennman Tunes Administered by Universal Music - Z Tunes LLC
All Rights for DWA Songs Administered by Almo Music Corp.
All Rights for MXM Administered Worldwide by Kobalt Songs Music Publishing
International Copyright Secured   All Rights Reserved

GRENADE

Violins

Words and Music by BRUNO MARS,
ARI LEVINE, PHILIP LAWRENCE,
BRODY BROWN, CLAUDE KELLY
and ANDREW WYATT

Moderately

© 2010 BMG FIREFLY, MARSFORCE MUSIC, BMG GOLD SONGS, TOY PLANE MUSIC, ROUND HILL SONGS,
WARNER-TAMERLANE PUBLISHING CORP., STUDIO BEAST MUSIC, NORTHSIDE INDEPENDENT MUSIC PUBLISHING LLC, THOU ART THE HUNGER,
WESTSIDE INDEPENDENT MUSIC PUBLISHING LLC, LATE 80'S MUSIC, WB MUSIC CORP., ROC NATION MUSIC,
MUSIC FAMAMANEM and DOWNTOWN COPYRIGHT MANAGEMENT LLC
This arrangement © 2017 BMG FIREFLY, MARSFORCE MUSIC, BMG GOLD SONGS, TOY PLANE MUSIC, ROUND HILL SONGS,
WARNER-TAMERLANE PUBLISHING CORP., STUDIO BEAST MUSIC, NORTHSIDE INDEPENDENT MUSIC PUBLISHING LLC, THOU ART THE HUNGER,
WESTSIDE INDEPENDENT MUSIC PUBLISHING LLC, LATE 80'S MUSIC, WB MUSIC CORP., ROC NATION MUSIC,
MUSIC FAMAMANEM and DOWNTOWN COPYRIGHT MANAGEMENT LLC
All Rights for BMG FIREFLY, MARSFORCE MUSIC, BMG GOLD SONGS, TOY PLANE MUSIC and ROUND HILL SONGS
Administered by BMG RIGHTS MANAGEMENT (US) LLC
All Rights for STUDIO BEAST MUSIC Administered by WARNER-TAMERLANE PUBLISHING CORP.
All Rights for THOU ART THE HUNGER Administered by NORTHSIDE INDEPENDENT MUSIC PUBLISHING LLC
All Rights for LATE 80'S MUSIC Administered by WESTSIDE INDEPENDENT MUSIC PUBLISHING LLC
All Rights for ROC NATION MUSIC and MUSIC FAMAMANEM Administered by WB MUSIC CORP.
All Rights Reserved   Used by Permission

HEY, SOUL SISTER

VIOLINS

Words and Music by PAT MONAHAN,
ESPEN LIND and AMUND BJORKLUND

Copyright © 2009 EMI April Music Inc., Blue Lamp Music and Stellar Songs Ltd.
This arrangement Copyright © 2017 EMI April Music Inc., Blue Lamp Music and Stellar Songs Ltd.
All Rights Administered by Sony/ATV Music Publishing LLC, 424 Church Street, Suite 1200, Nashville, TN 37219
International Copyright Secured   All Rights Reserved

HOME

VIOLINS

Words and Music by GREG HOLDEN
and DREW PEARSON

© 2012 FALLEN ART MUSIC, DREWYEAH MUSIC and SONGS OF PULSE RECORDING
This arrangement © 2017 FALLEN ART MUSIC, DREWYEAH MUSIC and SONGS OF PULSE RECORDING
All Rights for FALLEN ART MUSIC Administered by WB MUSIC CORP.
All Rights for DREWYEAH MUSIC Administered by SONGS OF PULSE RECORDING
All Rights Reserved   Used by Permission

I WILL WAIT

VIOLINS

Words and Music by
MUMFORD & SONS

Copyright © 2012 UNIVERSAL MUSIC PUBLISHING LTD.
This arrangement Copyright © 2017 UNIVERSAL MUSIC PUBLISHING LTD.
All Rights in the U.S. and Canada Controlled and Administered by UNIVERSAL - POLYGRAM INTERNATIONAL TUNES, INC.
All Rights Reserved   Used by Permission

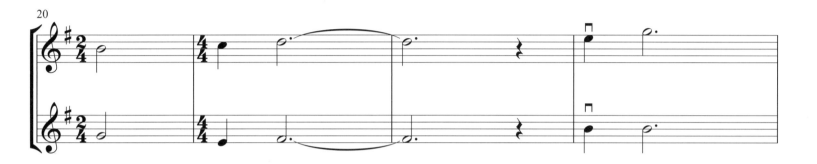

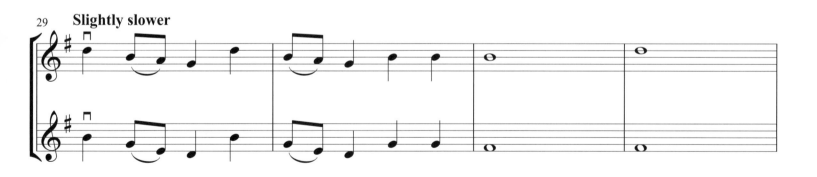

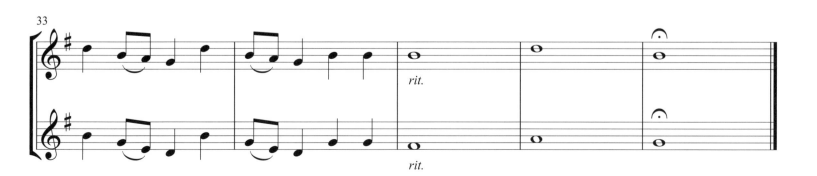

LET HER GO

VIOLINS

Words and Music by
MICHAEL DAVID ROSENBERG

Copyright © 2012 Sony/ATV Music Publishing (UK) Limited
This arrangement Copyright © 2017 Sony/ATV Music Publishing (UK) Limited
All Rights Administered by Sony/ATV Music Publishing LLC, 424 Church Street, Suite 1200, Nashville, TN 37219
International Copyright Secured   All Rights Reserved

LET IT GO

VIOLINS

Words and Music by JAMES BAY
and PAUL BARRY

Copyright © 2014 Spirit B-Unique Music and Metrophonic Music Ltd.
This arrangement Copyright © 2017 Spirit B-Unique Music and Metrophonic Music Ltd.
All Rights for Spirit B-Unique Music Administered Worldwide by Songs Of Kobalt Music Publishing
All Rights for Metrophonic Music Ltd. in the U.S. and Canada Administered by Universal - PolyGram International Publishing, Inc.
All Rights Reserved   Used by Permission

100 YEARS

VIOLINS

Words and Music by
JOHN ONDRASIK

Copyright © 2003 Five For Fighting Music
This arrangement Copyright © 2017 Five For Fighting Music
All Rights Administered Worldwide by Songs Of Kobalt Music Publishing
All Rights Reserved   Used by Permission

POKER FACE

VIOLINS

Words and Music by STEFANI GERMANOTTA
and RedOne

Copyright © 2008 Sony/ATV Music Publishing LLC, House Of Gaga Publishing Inc. and RedOne Productions, LLC
This arrangement Copyright © 2017 Sony/ATV Music Publishing LLC, House Of Gaga Publishing Inc. and RedOne Productions, LLC
All Rights Administered by Sony/ATV Music Publishing LLC, 424 Church Street, Suite 1200, Nashville, TN 37219
International Copyright Secured   All Rights Reserved

ROYALS

VIOLINS

Words and Music by ELLA YELICH-O'CONNOR
and JOEL LITTLE

Copyright © 2012, 2013 Songs Music Publishing, LLC o/b/o Songs Of SMP and EMI April Music Inc.
This arrangement Copyright © 2017 Songs Music Publishing, LLC o/b/o Songs Of SMP and EMI April Music Inc.
All Rights on behalf of EMI April Music Inc. Administered by Sony/ATV Music Publishing LLC, 424 Church Street, Suite 1200, Nashville, TN 37219
All Rights Reserved   Used by Permission

(small note optional)

SAY SOMETHING

VIOLINS

Words and Music by IAN AXEL,
CHAD VACCARINO and MIKE CAMPBELL

Copyright © 2011 SONGS OF UNIVERSAL, INC., IAN AXEL MUSIC, CHAD VACCARINO PUBLISHING, MANHATTAN ASTRONAUT MUSIC and RESERVOIR 416
This arrangement Copyright © 2017 SONGS OF UNIVERSAL, INC., IAN AXEL MUSIC,
CHAD VACCARINO PUBLISHING, MANHATTAN ASTRONAUT MUSIC and RESERVOIR 416
All Rights for IAN AXEL MUSIC and CHAD VACCARINO PUBLISHING Controlled and Administered by SONGS OF UNIVERSAL, INC.
All Rights for MANHATTAN ASTRONAUT MUSIC and RESERVOIR 416 Administered by RESERVOIR MEDIA MANAGEMENT, INC.
All Rights Reserved   Used by Permission

SHAKE IT OFF

VIOLINS

Words and Music by TAYLOR SWIFT,
MAX MARTIN and SHELLBACK

Copyright © 2014 Sony/ATV Music Publishing LLC, Taylor Swift Music and MXM
This arrangement Copyright © 2017 Sony/ATV Music Publishing LLC, Taylor Swift Music and MXM
All Rights on behalf of Sony/ATV Music Publishing LLC and Taylor Swift Music Administered by
Sony/ATV Music Publishing LLC, 424 Church Street, Suite 1200, Nashville, TN 37219
All Rights on behalf of MXM Administered Worldwide by Kobalt Songs Music Publishing
International Copyright Secured   All Rights Reserved

SHAPE OF YOU

VIOLINS

Words and Music by ED SHEERAN,
KEVIN BRIGGS, KANDI BURRUSS,
TAMEKA COTTLE, STEVE MAC
and JOHNNY McDAID

Copyright © 2017 Sony/ATV Music Publishing (UK) Limited, EMI April Music Inc., Air Control Music, Kandacy Music, Tiny Tam Music,
Shek'em Down Music, Pepper Drive Music, Tony Mercedes Music, Rokstone Music and Spirit B-Unique Polar Patrol
This arrangement Copyright © 2017 Sony/ATV Music Publishing (UK) Limited, EMI April Music Inc., Air Control Music, Kandacy Music, Tiny Tam Music,
Shek'em Down Music, Pepper Drive Music, Tony Mercedes Music, Rokstone Music and Spirit B-Unique Polar Patrol
All Rights on behalf of Sony/ATV Music Publishing (UK) Limited, EMI April Music Inc., Air Control Music, Kandacy Music
and Tiny Tam Music Administered by Sony/ATV Music Publishing LLC, 424 Church Street, Suite 1200, Nashville, TN 37219
All Rights on behalf of Shek'em Down Music Administered by Songs Of Windswept Pacific and Hitco Music
All Rights on behalf of Songs Of Windswept Pacific and Hitco Music Administered by BMG Rights Management (US) LLC
All Rights on behalf of Pepper Drive Music Administered by Warner-Tamerlane Publishing Corp.
All Rights on behalf of Tony Mercedes Music Administered by WB Music Corp.
All Rights on behalf of Rokstone Music in the United States and Canada Administered by Universal - PolyGram International Publishing, Inc.
All Rights on behalf of Spirit B-Unique Polar Patrol Controlled and Administered by Spirit B-Unique Polar Patrol Songs
International Copyright Secured   All Rights Reserved
- contains samples of "No Scrubs" by Kevin Briggs, Kandi Burruss and Tameka Cottle © 1999 EMI April Music Inc.,
Air Control Music, Kandacy Music, Tiny Tam Music, Shek'em Down Music, Pepper Drive Music and Tony Mercedes Music

SKYFALL
from the Motion Picture SKYFALL

VIOLINS

Words and Music by ADELE ADKINS
and PAUL EPWORTH

Copyright © 2012 MELTED STONE PUBLISHING LTD. and EMI MUSIC PUBLISHING LTD.
This arrangement Copyright © 2017 MELTED STONE PUBLISHING LTD. and EMI MUSIC PUBLISHING LTD.
All Rights for MELTED STONE PUBLISHING LTD. in the U.S. and Canada Controlled and Administered by
UNIVERSAL - SONGS OF POLYGRAM INTERNATIONAL, INC.
All Rights for EMI MUSIC PUBLISHING LTD. Administered by SONY/ATV MUSIC PUBLISHING LLC, 424 Church Street, Suite 1200, Nashville, TN 37219
All Rights Reserved   Used by Permission

SOME NIGHTS

VIOLINS

Words and Music by JEFF BHASKER,
ANDREW DOST, JACK ANTONOFF
and NATE RUESS

Copyright © 2012 Sony/ATV Music Publishing LLC, Way Above Music, Rough Art, Shira Lee Lawrence Rick Music, WB Music Corp., FBR Music and Bearvon Music
This arrangement Copyright © 2017 Sony/ATV Music Publishing LLC, Way Above Music, Rough Art,
Shira Lee Lawrence Rick Music, WB Music Corp., FBR Music and Bearvon Music
All Rights on behalf of Sony/ATV Music Publishing LLC, Way Above Music, Rough Art and Shira Lee Lawrence Rick Music Administered by
Sony/ATV Music Publishing LLC, 424 Church Street, Suite 1200, Nashville, TN 37219
All Rights on behalf of FBR Music and Bearvon Music Administered by WB Music Corp.
International Copyright Secured   All Rights Reserved

STAY WITH ME

VIOLINS

Words and Music by SAM SMITH,
JAMES NAPIER, WILLIAM EDWARD PHILLIPS,
TOM PETTY and JEFF LYNNE

Copyright © 2014 Sony/ATV Music Publishing (UK) Limited, Naughty Words Limited, Stellar Songs Ltd.,
Salli Isaak Songs Ltd., Method Paperwork Ltd., Gone Gator Music and EMI April Music Inc.
This arrangement Copyright © 2017 Sony/ATV Music Publishing (UK) Limited, Naughty Words Limited, Stellar Songs Ltd.,
Salli Isaak Songs Ltd., Method Paperwork Ltd., Gone Gator Music and EMI April Music Inc.
All Rights on behalf of Sony/ATV Music Publishing (UK) Limited, Naughty Words Limited, Stellar Songs Ltd. and EMI April Music Inc. Administered by
Sony/ATV Music Publishing LLC, 424 Church Street, Suite 1200, Nashville, TN 37219
All Rights on behalf of Salli Isaak Songs Ltd. and Method Paperwork Ltd. in the U.S. and Canada Administered by Universal - PolyGram International Tunes, Inc.
International Copyright Secured   All Rights Reserved

STORY OF MY LIFE

VIOLINS

Words and Music by JAMIE SCOTT,
JOHN HENRY RYAN, JULIAN BUNETTA,
HARRY STYLES, LIAM PAYNE, LOUIS TOMLINSON,
NIALL HORAN and ZAIN MALIK

Copyright © 2013 EMI Music Publishing Ltd., BMG Platinum Songs, Music Of Big Deal, The Family Songbook, Bob Erotik Music, Holy Cannoli Music and PPM Music Ltd.
This arrangement Copyright © 2017 EMI Music Publishing Ltd., BMG Platinum Songs, Music Of Big Deal,
The Family Songbook, Bob Erotik Music, Holy Cannoli Music and PPM Music Ltd.
All Rights on behalf of EMI Music Publishing Ltd. Administered by Sony/ATV Music Publishing LLC, 424 Church Street, Suite 1200, Nashville, TN 37219
All Rights on behalf of BMG Platinum Songs, Music Of Big Deal, The Family Songbook and Bob Erotik Music Administered by BMG Rights Management (US) LLC
All Rights on behalf of Holy Cannoli Music Administered by Songs Of Universal, Inc.
All Rights on behalf of PPM Music Ltd. Administered by Downtown DLJ Songs
International Copyright Secured   All Rights Reserved

VIVA LA VIDA

VIOLINS

Words and Music by GUY BERRYMAN,
JON BUCKLAND, WILL CHAMPION
and CHRIS MARTIN

Copyright © 2008 by Universal Music Publishing MGB Ltd.
This arrangement Copyright © 2017 by Universal Music Publishing MGB Ltd.
All Rights in the United States and Canada Administered by Universal Music - MGB Songs
International Copyright Secured   All Rights Reserved

HAL LEONARD PRESENTS

EASY INSTRUMENTAL DUETS

Start your duet playing experience with these fun songbooks! Over 20 easy duet arrangements for two instrumentalists are featured in each of these collections. Woodwind and brass editions can be played together as can the string editions. **Only $9.99 each!**

BROADWAY SONGS FOR TWO

22 showstoppers: Any Dream Will Do • Bring Him Home • Cabaret • Edelweiss • For Forever • Hello, Dolly! • I Believe • Memory • One • Popular • Seasons of Love • Seventy Six Trombones • Tomorrow • Where Is Love? • You've Got a Friend • and more.

00252493 FLUTE
00252494 CLARINET
00252495 ALTO SAX
00252496 TRUMPET
00252497 TROMBONE
00252500 VIOLIN
00252501 CELLO

CLASSICAL THEMES FOR TWO

24 favorite melodies from top classical composers: Air on the G String • Blue Danube Waltz • Canon in D • Eine Kleine Nachtmusik • Hallelujah Chorus • Jesu, Joy of Man's Desiring • Minuet in G Major • Ode to Joy • Pictures at an Exhibition • Sheep May Safely Graze • Trumpet Voluntary • William Tell Overture • and more.

00254439 FLUTE
00254440 CLARINET
00254441 ALTO SAX
00254442 TRUMPET
00254443 TROMBONE
00254444 VIOLIN
00254445 CELLO

CHRISTMAS HITS FOR TWO

22 terrific holiday duets: All I Want for Christmas Is You • Baby, It's Cold Outside • The Christmas Song (Chestnuts Roasting on an Open Fire) • Do You Want to Build a Snowman? • Feliz Navidad • Have Yourself a Merry Little Christmas • It's Beginning to Look like Christmas • Let It Snow! Let It Snow! Let It Snow! • Mary, Did You Know? • Rockin' Around the Christmas Tree • Silver Bells • White Christmas • and more.

00172461 FLUTE
00172462 CLARINET
00172463 ALTO SAX
00172464 TRUMPET
00172465 TROMBONE
00172466 VIOLIN
00172467 CELLO

HIT SONGS FOR TWO

22 mega hits: All About That Bass • All of Me • Brave • Can't Stop the Feeling • Grenade • Hey, Soul Sister • I Will Wait • Let Her Go • 100 Years • Royals • Shake It Off • Shape of You • Stay with Me • Viva La Vida • and more.

00252482 FLUTE
00252483 CLARINET
00252484 ALTO SAX
00252485 TRUMPET
00252486 TROMBONE
00252487 VIOLIN
00252488 CELLO

Prices, contents and availability subject to change without notice.
Sales restrictions to some countries apply.
All prices listed in U.S. funds.

ORDER TODAY FROM YOUR FAVORITE MUSIC
RETAILER AT **HALLEONARD.COM**